Girl in the mirror

by

Alicja Maria Kuberska

Augur Press

GIRL IN THE MIRROR

Copyright © Alicja Maria Kuberska 2015

The moral right of the author has been asserted

British Library Cataloguing in Publication Data.
A catalogue record for this book is available from
the British Library.

ISBN 978-0-9571380-8-7

First published 2015 by
Augur Press
Delf House
52 Penicuik Road
Roslin
Midlothian EH25 9LH
United Kingdom

Printed by Lightning Source

Girl in the mirror

For my family and friends, and everyone who has been involved in the production of this collection.

Contents

Preface

About the author

Preface

In these poems, Alicja harnesses her striking abilities in ways that prepare the reader's mind for deeper reflection.

She uses highly refined qualities of perception and insight, enabling us to conceptualise hitherto unconscious aspects of our experience, or to re-enter and explore areas that we have already formed. She applies her perception and insight to many different phases of life, in physical, emotional and spiritual realms.

Her own particular use of words to convey thoughts, ideas and concepts demonstrates skills and gifts that are remarkable.

Each poem manifests almost as a meditation – on an aspect of life, or on life itself. Although each can be absorbed entirely separately, every one has an equal power and impact when connected to the others. Alone, each conveys its own message, and together they speak as companions mingling to create a single voice.

Girl in the mirror

Smile
Sad girl in the mirror.
Yesterday you worried about tomorrow.
Today is full of miracles.

Is every morning grey?

Look!
For you the dawn radiates colour
Large clouds of pink and white.
Make friends with every hour
And discover the colours of moments.

(Not) my poem

I wrote a few words and linked them together
Reflections and emotions created an immaterial line.
I uttered the last phrase and he moved like a zephyr,
Kissing my lips lightly as he left, gliding away to strangers.

He slipped into their eyes where tears are born
He whispered beautiful words to their hearts,
  and they quivered tenderly.
He awoke their sleeping consciences, bored by daily routine.
He consoled a very sad lady, Melancholy.

At night he flew into the sky, parting heavy curtains of clouds.
The stars glittered and the moon lit up the paths of lovers.
The tender song of a nightingale mingled with him
  in the abyss of darkness
And sunk into the exquisite swooning scent of flowers.

Sometimes this unfaithful lover returns to me
Beloved son of the muse, not my child any more.

Drawers

Large drawers
Fat dragons with big bellies
Protect the fragments of my poems.

Careless letters saved,
Scraps, snippets of thoughts, dreams, emotions
On which I have been musing.
Scrambled notes
About what is needed and what is not.
Napkins from a bar,
Small pieces of paper
Lie dormant.

Maybe someday
I will open the drawer.
From the chrysalis of pages
Poems will emerge, as colourful as dragonflies
Or might jump out like crickets, chirping.
And they will fly, who knows where
And to whom?

At daybreak

Wake me up
Delicately, and with tenderness.
Blow away the dream
From my eyelashes.

Then I will see
How Aurora with her rose fingers
Slices through the darkness of the night
And lightens the blue of the sky.
All birds, in their tree havens
Sing the hymn that heralds dawn.

The first warm rays of the sun
Will kiss the petals of sleeping flowers.
This is the miracle of a new day created.

Good morning

The train

I entered the train of life
With nothing.
Without clothes
Without feelings.
A blank sheet of paper.
Blotting paper, absorbing everything.

I will alight burdened with bundles of
Recollections and impressions.
I had packed these carefully.
Some of them are faded, like ink from old letters.

I had tied them with ribbons of all colours.
White ones denote
My inessential memories
And black ones signify heaviness and trauma.

I met many passengers
Throughout this long journey
And free-riders too,
Who were picked up along the way.

Each meeting,
Even the shortest one,
Like a flash of sun or flutter of butterfly wings
Filled and enriched my store of experiences.

Dew

I know
That I am as
A drop of dew
Hanging between
Night and day.

I know too
That I exist only
A short time
In this world.

I learn from yesterday
I live for today
I dream of tomorrow.

In the attic

A large spider senses its reflection in a dusty mirror.
It cast a dense veil,
  woven from white threads over the silver surface
And the world became blurred,
  with only contours being visible.

The time had stopped inside a broken grandfather clock.
Silent, trapped between the many gears in its mechanism.
Twice a day, the spread hands show the time.

In the deep drawers of an old oak cupboard,
Black and white photographs
  of smiling, nameless people slumber.
They are not capable of telling long-forgotten tales.

Dresses, made of good-quality materials,
  hang in the creaking armoire.
Unfashionable, sentenced to inertia and the odour of mothballs,
  they dream about the sun.
Do they believe that someday their fortune will change
  and they will see the light?

Books with yellowed pages, dreaming inside old trunks,
Have incorporated the touch of many hands, teardrops,
  and reflections.
Occasionally they leave the attic
  to share their knowledge and sentiment.

Stones

I love stones,
Their history, structure and language.

People think that stones are hard,
Insensitive and introverted.

I see in them
The molten passion of lava and whirls of fire.

You have to know how to read them
To see what was, what is now and what will be.

Encounter with a stranger

We collided at the speed of light
And we stood, amazed.
This was such an unexpected meeting
In terms of logic it was hardly possible.

Maybe
We could have met in a bar at different tables,
Or passed indifferently on a street,
Or sat silently next to each other on the subway.

Certainly
We exchanged a few controversial views
And revealed some secret thoughts and dreams.

An honest conversation is easier
With a person without a face.

The meeting place

Our favourite bar exists in time and space.
Nothing changes there.
The floor, like a mirror, reflects lights
In shades of sky-blue and navy.

The bartender,
Trustee of love's mysteries,
With the face of a Sphinx,
Concocts love potions
Or collects tears in chalices.

I heard only your voice.
I held you by the hand.
Our fingers trembled eagerly.
I saw only your eyes.
We were alone in the crowd.
We found silence among sounds.

We can return here, where all began.
Let us write another episode of life.
Our barstools, like giraffes, will reach the sky.
The bartender will smile
And offer us another magic elixir.

Sometime in autumn

We walked in the park, hidden under an umbrella.
Thick fog imbued us with melancholy,
  and cold touched our hands.
Clouds, supporting the weight of the rain,
  hung low over the trees.
Puddles mirrored the reflections of lanterns,
  tired by the night vigil.

Suddenly the sun glimmered, and autumn smiled.
Trees discarded greyness in favour of colour.
Droplets of dew sparkled,
  and rusty chestnuts danced across the paths.
Yellow leaves, fragrant with moisture, twirled in the breeze.

You spoke quietly of love.
You spun words like threads of Indian summer.
I committed to memory vibrations of voice
  and the embrace of clasped fingers.
You held me,
And then you wove an engagement ring out of the grass
  … with a white daisy for the diamond.

Broken mirror

You closed the doors of words.
My heart trembled and fell down
Like a mirror from the wall.
It shattered, and lost some pieces.

People say
It is seven years of bad luck
And I think perhaps more.
I cannot glue it.
I tried.
Something is missing.

Thoughts and words carry a bitter taste
The world looks different now.

Another love

Love can be the enemy. The worst kind.
It can blur the contours of reality
And feed it with toxic illusions.
Cheques without value are paid for the future.

Love gives you tinted glasses
Tells you that the world is pastel.
It mocks the mind and leads it to the swamp
Where it strangles it in the sea of flowers.

There is no mercy when it leaves.
It takes its stand with miracles and dreams.
You are burnt in the fires of passion
And left in ruins.

The Flying Dutchman

I'm losing hope.
I close my eyes and fly in the air
Over unfulfilled promises.
I am pulling up the anchor, departing hastily.

My thoughts are rolled up, like sails in stormy weather.
Some of them are just tattered illusions
Waving sadly in the wind.

And it could be so beautiful… I reflect in loneliness.

I feel waves of disappointment breaking over me,
Drops of sea water wet my face, or maybe they are tears.
Feelings can have the destructive force of a tornado.
Dreams about a safe harbour
Vanished in a fog of helplessness and grief.

I do not know the meaning of the word 'peace'.
Distrust sentences me for another journey.
It is impossible to forget.
Do I dissolve in reality… becoming as nothing?

Request

Protect me,
Like a glowing candle,
Against the gusts of life.

Take care of me.
I will give you warmth and light.

Build a raft of your fingers.
Do not allow me to sink
Into sadness.

I am imperfect
In this almost perfect world.
Ever more frail, faulty and weak.

A few things

I forgot how little I need.
The lure of possession had deceived me.
I drank the colours and shapes of 'the next thing'.
I was like a bee, drinking nectar, but from poisonous plants.

Everyone said to me I would not be happy without.
I believed in the colourful adverts and posters shouting at me.
They portrayed a vision of beauty and satisfaction.

More and more, newer and 'better' items.
I sank into the mire of a thousand unnecessary items.

I stopped, turned back and changed into salt like Lot's wife.
It surprised me that I had to find my way back to the border
Between 'to have' and 'to be'.

Illusions

I'm sorry that I imagined you.
I created an unreal world
Answering the questions knocking at my mind
Uninvited.
I did not give you a chance.
Nights brought dreams, and days delusion.
I've been living in a dream, which like watercolours
Blurred the reality.

Will you open your mind?

I knocked at your mind.
'Let me in?' I asked.
'I have brought you something.
My crazy thoughts and dreams,
The works collected from
The oceans of creativity.
Look how pretty they are,
Even the smallest ones,
Smaller than grains of sand.'

'I do not want them,' you replied.
'My world is sterile,
Arranged and known.
Your every written poem
Can ruin my calm
Which was constructed over years.
The recognition can be painful
Because of its insolence and ignorance.
The questions wake up sleeping fears.
I prefer to stay safely in
Well known loneliness.'

The crystal tears

It is said that time cures all wounds
And that people are not irreplaceable.
Yet the emptiness and longing always stays.

The most difficult tears are those not cried.
They turn into transparent crystals and jab the memory.
The muted cry hangs on the edge of despair and helplessness.

Network of silence

Loneliness is a silence
Unseen in the world of noise and rush.

Do not cry.
You can say that it is cool and nice.
Find a shelter in a virtual world
To forget about the real one.

So many lonely people,
Who thirst for touch and warmth.
So many evenings and nights without spoken words.
So many dreams of intimacy
Woven on the web of the internet.

The beggar

I looked deeply into the eyes of a beggar,
And they told me his story.

The book of life is not closed.
It describes failures and mistakes at the beginning,
Then the monotonous days,
Struggling to survive in a hostile world.

The streets are like a swamp.
They draw in and do not let go.
They promise nothing.
They provide only rarely.

He must drift on the surface of existence
On a raft built from old cartons.

Rushing cars honk loudly.
Passers-by mutter disapprovingly.
Only sometimes someone throws a few coins into the tin box
Compassionately.

Reversal

You are asking for a meeting.
It's like watching a film running from the end.

Look!
Wind replaces the hat on the head of a passerby.
The overturned chair rights itself.
A bouquet of red roses falls into someone's hands.

A kiss
To greet you?
Or to say goodbye?

Duty

I am trapped in a labyrinth of duties
My life but a series of signposts
Directing commands
You must…
You should…
You ought…
You are not allowed…
It is your duty.

I would have liked to rise out of it all and escape.

I know now that the only thing I really *have* to do is to die.
Nothing more.

Little town

I walk along the streets of the town
Which I once loved.
Today, as if an indifferent stranger,
I barely recognise it.

There are no more old, hospitable aunts,
No more nosey neighbours hidden behind curtains,
Or brave men with stories of war.
They are gone.

Time has changed everything
Not only the people, houses, streets and trees.
It seems to me that it has even
Repainted the colour of the sky.

Sailing-ship

I know. You are tired.

Old ships should not sail on rough waters.
It is time to hide within the safety of harbour walls
While we tell your story to the children
And the crowds of visitors.

Sometimes it is only the cry of the gulls
That will remind you of days gone by.
Then you will miss the crashing waves,
The salty smell and the wild ocean.

Old age

In the era of fractal geometry
We aim at perfection.
People want to equal the gods.
There is no place for being old.

Is this God's unsuccessful work,
Carefully hidden
In the waiting room of death,
Where life is ending?

There, old age,
With twisted fingers
Wrinkled faces
And a toothless mouth
Awaits us.

November

November comes.
Rain clouds, like huge duvets, cover the grey sky.
Trees no longer whisper and the birds fall silent.
Only sometimes
Sad crows slash the silence with loud cawing.

At night, frost visits the fields, turning meadows pale grey.
The last colourful leaves disappear with the wind somewhere.
The naked birches sleep, dream winter dreams,
Patiently wait for the distant spring,
Silhouette darkly against the distant sky,
With the elegance of Corinthian columns.

A little angel

I will send you my angel.
Take care of him.

He is so small that
You can hide him
In your hand or
Deep in your heart.

Remember that my angel
Is nourished by your smiles,
Well-wishing words and
Good deeds.

Do not allow him to die from hunger.

About the author

Alicja Maria Kuberska was born in 1960 in Świebodzin, Poland. She now lives with her family in the spa town of Inowrocław. She works full-time for the local town hall. In her spare time, she does voluntary work for the Music Society Pro Arte and for the Society of Sister-Cities Inowrocław (Poland) and Bad Oyenhausen (Germany). She is involved in many charities, and of course, she writes.

In 2011 she published her first volume of poems, entitled: 'The Glass Reality'. Her second volume 'Analysis of Feelings' was published in 2012. The third collection 'Moments' was published in English in 2014, both in Poland and in the USA. In 2014 she also published a novel – 'Virtual Roses' – and another collection of poems 'On the Border of Dream'.

Her poems have been published in numerous anthologies and magazines in Poland, the USA, the UK, Canada, India and Australia. She was the featured poet of New Mirage Journal (USA) in the summer of 2011. Her poem 'Train' was nominated for the Pushcart Prize in 2011. In 2014, her poem was mentioned in the international competition, Nosside. Her poems are read on various radio programmes in Poland and in Belgium. She has given a large number of interviews for Polish and American magazines and newspapers.

Alicja has written 8 monodramas and a play for teenagers. The monodrama 'Cousin' won the first prize in Kołobrzeg in 2013.

Alicja is a member of the Polish Writers Association in Warsaw. She is one of two editors of an artistic-literary quarterly journal 'Metafora', published by Miniatura, Kraków.

Her poems are included in various online literary magazines, and can be viewed on her Facebook page.

For other titles from Augur Press
please visit

www.augurpress.com

www.ingramcontent.com/pod-product-compliance
Lightning Source LLC
Chambersburg PA
CBHW020813130626
46554CB00006B/2408